alive and thankful

—ᴡᴡ—

Life is a gift

lon cole

ISBN: 0692326480
ISBN 13: 9780692326480

ACKNOWLEDGEMENTS

This collection of poems resulting in a book "Alive and Thankful" comes directly out of the support and belief of many people who encouraged me along the way: First I want to share my deep love and gratitude for my family. Cris Cole my wife, is truly my rock, My son Alonzo and daughter, Heidi, and their families, who love me unconditionally. You inspire me each day to share my thoughts and feelings through poetry.

Thanks are also due to three good friends Roger Donaldson who was a great help on the computer, Dr. John Davis, and Dr. Jack Ehlen, who have been a great support and thank you for your kind words. I'd also like to acknowledge the Alzheimer's Association and all my friends there, especially Keri Pollock, and Bob Le Roy Thank you for asking me to share my verse and tell my story, along with opportunities to serve as a volunteer partner. Thank you for your support on this journey

I also want to thank Createspace.com for all your help in making this happen for me

Lon Cole.

INTRODUCTION

Inspired by his own unique experiences, Lon has kept records of his life in poetry and writing. Being an artist myself, I have truly admired his ability to express his emotions through his writing. It's never easy to convey feelings, and yet he does so with ease in his words. Each poem is like a window into a piece of his soul that has been far overshadowed by daily strength that he must demonstrate. I have come to learn, as you will after reading this book, that all of us can be taken to the depths of despair. All of us can be wounded, yet it is within us to rise from it and become stronger. Word after word, he continues to surprise me, as he so effortlessly portrays the most basic human emotions. From joy and peace to fear and loneliness, his poetry touches on the emotions that unite us all.

Even now, after being diagnosed with the terrible disease of Alzheimer's, he has found a way to buoy up those around him. After reading this work you will know that you can be alive and thankful. His most powerful voice will be the one you will hear as he connects with you through poetry.

Without question, I know that his poetry, his attitude, and simply his presence among those who suffer from this disease, directly and indirectly, are strengthened by him

It is an honor to be his daughter. Life will give to all of us what we need to grow stronger, and he has taught that our very purpose on this earth is to love our families and our fellowman and to enjoy every minute of this life!

Heidi Grace Kress
June 2014

FOREWARD

My father was diagnosed with Alzheimer's disease fifteen years ago this week. He's 97, a slight, gentle, confused man, near—but not yet at—the end of a long and well-lived life.

But what about those whose journeys with Alzheimer's disease and related dementias are just beginning? Who will be there for them with help and hope as they struggle to cope with their uncertain and unwelcome futures?

At the Western and Central Washington State Chapter, we are taking steps to engage and serve this emerging and rapidly growing early stage population. "Early stage" refers to people, irrespective of age, who have been diagnosed with Alzheimer's disease or related dementia and are in the early stages of the disease. In this stage, individuals retain the ability to participate in daily activities and a give-and-take dialogue. This group includes individuals with "younger onset" Alzheimer's—under age 65 and still in the early stages of the disease.

One of the key objectives in our current strategic plan is to "be an early and ongoing point of contact for people diagnosed with Alzheimer's disease, either directly or through a caregiver". To achieve this objective for persons with dementia and their care partners, we:

- Added an Early Stage Memory Loss Coordinator to our staff to engage and serve our early stage client base utilizing a "best practices" approach to integrate elements of successful programs currently in use across the Association

- Host eight early stage support groups

- Recruited an early stage advisory council of persons with dementia and their care partners to guide us in the assessment, development, and enhancement of our early stage outreach

- Launched a "peer to peer" program linking trained volunteers with dementia to newly-diagnosed individuals for ongoing education and support

- Collaborate with the Frye Art Museum on the "here: now" program of arts engagement

- Collaborate with Seattle Parks and Recreation on a weekly walking program at the Woodland Park Zoo

No one personifies the diligence and determination, energy and effort, heart and humor of our early stage outreach quite like Lon Cole. Lon and his wife, Chris, attend an early stage support group. He serves on our Early Stage Advisory Council and our Pierce County Regional Advisory Council. He is a peer-to-peer counselor. He is our Chapter's poet laureate!

Lon's poetry is truly the window to his soul. In *Alive and Thankful*, he opens that window for all of us, guides us through heartache to hope, reminds us what we mean to one another and of our better selves, and leaves us feeling *"alive and thankful"*.

Three of Lon's poems have special meaning for me:

- *My Partner* is a valentine to a life partner. I shared it with my wife on our wedding anniversary two weeks ago.

> *Now you're with me always*
> *Wherever I may go*
> *The love that we both honor*
> *Will fill my lonely soul*

- *Where am I going?* urges us to hold tight to the gift of life.

> *I'll look for tomorrow and live for today*
> *And hold to the good as it passes my way*
> *I'm strong to the challenge and must be sincere*
> *For life is a gift, so precious and dear*

- *The Visions We Share* is a life-affirming response to growing old.

> *The visions we share are simple today*
> *That is because we need them that way*
> *You're only as old as your heart wants to be*
> *So live all you can and learn to be free*

Lon honors us with his poetry and his service. I'm proud to say that he honors me with his friendship. At the Alzheimer's Association, we offer help and hope. Our vision is a world without Alzheimer's disease. With partners like Lon, we are in very good company.

...Bob

Bob Le Roy
President and Chief Executive Officer
Alzheimer's Association
Western & Central Washington State Chapter
100 W Harrison Street, North Tower, Suite 200
Seattle WA 98119
206-529-3891 (Office)
206-363-5700 (Fax)
206-498-4131 (Cell)
bleroy@alz.org

TABLE OF CONTENTS

ALIVE AND THANKFUL

Some days are good days
Some days are bad
I want to be happy
I want to feel glad

I wish I could remember
Like I used to before
And treasure those moments
That made my heart sing and soar

The names and the faces
I knew everyone
And now there a puzzle
Each memory is gone

I haven't forgotten
How to laugh or to cry
Or say I'm alive and thankful
When someone walks by

Things aren't so bad
They could probably be worse
But I count my blessings
And consider the source

THE GOOD TIMES

Most of our friends and the people we know
Only see our good sides—that's all we will show

We have many habits, both good and bad
Some make us happy; some make us sad

We want to treat everyone with the best of care
In hopes that our friendships will always be there

We have lived good lives, as good as can be
The places we go and the people we see

There's so much to remember and so much to do
We look to the past and hold to the new

All the things we have done can puzzle the brain
It can give us a headache or drive us insane

The good times are there for you and for me
We must listen softly and be ready to see

A Bond Is a Friendship

You are the ones that know how I feel
Our bond is like friendship, and ever so real

We crossed the same path, but were never alone
Though it often seemed we were all on our own

A call or a visit goes a long way
To make us all stronger, and brighten our days

We must hold together, the reason is clear
In sharing our challenge we need not fear

And whether together or far apart
Our bond is not weakened, but strengthens our heart

A Dark Way to Go

I depend on the Lord to get me though
The challenges of life and what they can do

Dementia is a dark way to go
It creeps up behind you and takes you so slow

You first start forgetting, your short-term memory fails
From that time on, it's an ugly dark trail

There's still time to reason, to love, and to plan
To teach those that love you, and help them understand

Now when you get worse, you won't know it by then
There's no need to worry when you come to your end

A Daughter's Calling

I have a daughter, an incredible girl,
Who is bigger than life, like a precious pearl

She can be whatever she chooses to be
The calling she has chosen is to be the mother of three

Such a noble way to live her life
A devoted mother, and a loving wife

I'm sure her adventures will not end
And she will be challenged again and again

A Good Night Rest

Are you waiting for a reason to close your eyes at night?
Do you long for peaceful sleep to rest your weary sight?

What keeps us awake so long when we want to fall asleep?
The mind gets so restless; you sleep shallow instead of deep

How long can someone go on without the proper rest?
Your head starts to throb and you get a pain deep in your chest

Sleep is so important—it stops us from losing our minds
It gives us a chance to process our thoughts and also a way to unwind

Can we go on without any sleep? It's impossible for us to do
If you start to go insane a good rest is the only thing for you

So close your eyes and hope for the best
Your brain will take over and do all the rest

When you wake up, your body will feel great
Especially if you chose to sleep in late

A Holy Place

The temple is truly a holy place
It can lift you up from the troubles you face

When you attend, you feel the spirit inside
In the temple there's no room for envy or false pride

It helps you feel humble, peaceful, and meek,
Yet there's a power that can shatter the weak

As you listen to its message your soul becomes strong
It's there to remind you to avoid anger and wrong

Return to the temple as often as you can
There is so much to learn and understand

So enter the temple to worship the Lord
You'll gain much wisdom and should never get bored

A Lasting Friendship

Real friendship is a gift from God
That comes to only a few
I thank the Lord for sending us
The dearest of friends like you

And when life is really tough on us all
And we were feeling so down
The friends we've grown to love so much
Always seemed to be around

And though are faiths may differ
Our purpose is the same
To share a lasting friendship
I'm truly proud to claim

A New Year Comes

Every time a new year comes
Excitement fills the air
We set our goals the best we can
And try to make them fair

The family gets excited
Everyone knows the time is near
Each task set is a challenge
And failure becomes the fear

Now when the task is finished.
All feel the joy of success
This makes them want to shout
And wipe away their stress

A new year brings you victory
A feeling we must know
It drives away the loneliness
And makes the heart start to glow

A New Year Will Start

It's Christmastime and there is no need to fear
Look forward to the joy of the upcoming new year

If you are happy when the new year begins
You will have no remorse when the old year ends

What will you do to change the new year?
You must erase all your worries and ban all your fears

Are you looking forward to all you can do?
Will all of your dreams start to come true?

Was last year a good year? Did everything go right?
Or was it filled with the darkness of a cold lonely night?

I'm sure there will be surprises as the year moves along
You must keep the faith when something goes wrong

Time never stops; no day is the same
If that's not the case it would really be a shame

A Small Little Seed

It's hard to control anger when it's all you see
If anger controls you, you'll never be free

Anger can grow from a small little seed
But the blossom that springs will just be a weed

How can you turn the wrath of anger away?
It's not that easy—that's all I can say

I guess the best way is to dwell on peace
You must suffocate anger or it will increase

Don't say to yourself I have no control
You can beat your mind—that's all you must know

Peace is the goal that you must obtain
If you get rid of your anger, Joy will remain

A Special and Sacred Time

Christmas is a time when we want our family near
It's a magical time that's filled with holiday cheer

Children start to dream of getting Santa's toys
As the joy of laughter fills every girl and boy

Great things happen on this wonderful day
People are kinder in what they do and say

We try to serve others, especially those in need
To give of ourselves as we do our rightly deeds

Christmas is a special and sacred time of year
We learn to help others and relinquish all our fears

If we could emulate the Lord for just a little while
This world that we share would be filled with far less guile

So celebrate his birthday like we all should
Give all you can to others and try to be really good

A Trip to the Doctor

I went to the doctor the story is told
Just take a few tests, that's the bill I was sold

Four hours later they were all done
All I can say is it wasn't much fun

We will get back to you in one to two weeks
It took much longer—my future must be bleak

Come down to see us and get the results of your test
There's no need to worry if you gave it your best

We sat in the office as the two of them came in
No one was smiling, not even a grin

I told them a joke; I thought they would laugh
No one was laughing, not one of the staff

So what are the results, can you tell me please?
I'm afraid we must tell you that you have Alzheimer's disease

What could I say or what could I do?
We sat pretty quiet until they were through

We climbed in the car and headed for home
We weren't feeling good we thought we were all on our own

But then I remembered some thing the doctor had said
It got me to start thinking while I was in bed

I got up in the middle of the night
I went to the kitchen and turned on the light

I made one phone call while rubbing my eyes
And a real person answered to my surprise

She answered my questions—every single one
I felt so much better when we were all done

Now I'm happy with where I must go
Especially to hear that the progression is slow

The Alzheimer's Association is a very good group
They won't let you down, and they'll jump through the hoops

A Voice Can Be Heard

Your voice can be heard if you want it to be
It matters what you do and say
Others may hear something of value
Something that they can carry away

The most important thing is to speak from the heart
Though it's hard to do sometimes
When you do, the trueness comes out,
your spirit starts to climb

If it helps only one, it's worth it I feel
For doing good can't be measured in deeds
The thought from a soul has infinite worth
It helps others want to succeed

So speak how you feel in a tender way
Hold strong to your will and your mind
When others need help, be there for them
Speak boldly but always be kind

A Weary Mind

My mind longs for clarity
It's pureness that I seek
All I have are fog and clouds,
Which make my mind so weak

I try to think of what to do
To help my consciousness awake
I've been on hold for too long
Afraid my brain will break

I had such wisdom long before
Recalling was such an ease
Now it's blank in every way
Can someone help me please?

I need it back, what I have lost
Just help me if you can
Turn on the inside of my head
That gets me to understand

Without Reward

Giving is an act of love
That the Lord would always do
When we give without reward
Our blessings are never through

Where, when, or how we give
Is not as important as why
In giving all that we can in life
It's worth more than money can buy

Everyone needs to help in some way
In doing so, our spirits climb
Helping others who can't help themselves
Is a wise way to spend money, talents, and time.

You should honor your service
By being as generous as you can
Whatever you give is worth more than you have
There is joy in giving others a helping hand

ALL ON YOUR OWN

When you feel you're all on your own
Try to remember you are not alone

Though you may be lonely and feeling blue
There's always someone that cares about you

Those little sad feelings you have inside
If you're not careful, they can grow to be wide

Reach out to others whenever you can
They are there to help you to understand

Don't let the darkness surround you complete
Sadness and depression can always be beat

A smile is the protection you might need
It can be ever growing like a beautiful seed

Always have a happy thought stored away
So you are prepared for a dark rainy day

Always Be Clean

Always be clean in both body and mind
Respect the freedom of others and try to be kind

Dirty jokes and bad language won't get you anywhere
A pure heart is priceless—it shows how you care

Be neat in appearance; don't look like a slob
Dress the best that you can when you show up for a job

Be clean while your working or just having fun
You don't need to be wealthy or know everyone

Good personal hygiene will go along way
It helps you feel happy no matter what others may say

Surround yourself with people who have values like you
Encourage them to be clean in all that they do

Always Have a Plan

Are you prepared and willing to fight each and every day?
As you seek, you're sure to find your solutions in every way

You must get help from others—what else can you do?
They will join you in your battles until the war is through

Each time you fight for goodness and peace everywhere
The Lord will walk beside you, your worries he will share

Take the giant steps forward; never slow yourself down
Moving, always moving, wear a smile not a frown

Take the lead in everything; be as humble as you can
Be organized in all you do and always have a plan

When you succeed in your final goal, be thankful to everyone
Without their help your mission could not be done

Especially, thank the Lord above; his blessings helped you soar
When you are called on again, you will need him even more

ARMS OPEN WIDE

I am a caregiver
I'm someone who cares;
When others are gone
I promise to be there.

I know it won't be easy
The pain I'll share with you;
I hope it will be worth it
In all I want to do.

There will be times I feel helpless
When I think I can't endure;
I pray that you'll forgive me
My intentions will be pure.

I will not stand alone
The Lord is on our side;
He will be there when we need him
With his arms open wide.

When your journey is over
I know we will meet again;
Until that time must come
I'll be with you to the end.

As My Memory Fails

Do I remember?
Will he always be there?
Why must I forget?
It seems so unfair

Will I recall
All the many details?
Does time fade away
As my memory fails?

What will I treasure
When my senses are gone?
Will others connect
Or will they move on?

How will I get there?
When will I go?
I wish it would move faster
But the trip seems so slow

Help me believe
That hope is still near
I can't give up
No matter how much I fear

Give me a chance
To find my own way
I might be ready
In just a few days

I must accept
What lies before me
The darker it gets
The less I feel free

I'll search for the light
No matter how far
I know it is near
Much brighter than a star

How do you say goodbye
To all those you love
Know God will be near
As he reigns from above

Assisted Living

Life is sure a blessing
What more could we ask
Every day is a challenge
There's always another task

When we achieve tasks
We feel really good
It's great to get things done
The right way as they should

We keep moving on
When jobs come our way
There is no fear now
It's sure to be okay

Now if I forget something
Someone will be there
To see to all my problems
And show me that they care

I am never alone now
There's always another who is near
To lighten my dark spirits
And fill my glass with cheer

I know they will care for me
When I am in need
And when I get slower
There will be no need for speed

Be All You Can Be

I don't know what people see in me
Maybe it's that I try to be all I can be

Give it your best, then a little bit more
Open your mind and your heart so you can soar

Learn from your lessons before it's too late
Do your best and you'll rule your own fate

Share with others the wisdom you learn
Take responsibility when it is your turn

Be cautious when questioned and answer sincere
If you tell the truth there is nothing to fear

Respect someone's freedom as if it were your own
Be wise in your spending avoid taking loans

All that I've said is just common sense
Stay on your path; don't jump the fence

Be Humble and True

Live your life; be humble and true
Make the right choices in all that you do

Acknowledge the Lord who helps you each day
And don't be puffed up when it's your turn to pray

Humility is a trait we all must learn
Be willing to help when it is your turn

Don't go on living like you're the only one
Be there for others till your duty is done

Don't fight to be the first one in line
Share what you have and try to be kind

Be quiet as you worship and don't make a scene
Go long without anger and keep your thoughts clean

BE ON THE RIGHT SIDE

Look to be positive, and be ready to show
The bright side is better—that's where you should go

Beware of the darkness; it's always near by
God's light shines brighter and pierces the eyes

There's a power in being positive in all that you do
Like being an A student helps you in school

Be on the right side and follow the Lord's path
He will keep you safe and away from Satan's wrath

Look at yourself as good not bad
Hold to the rod; it will help you feel glad

There is a great power for all of us to see
If we think the right way, it will set us free

Be Sure

I wish there was a way we could educate all
We could help everyone see the large picture instead of the small

Some make decisions with far too few facts
Then they decide and are quick to react

The use of the power to control someone's health
Can impact one's future far greater than wealth

You must try to be sure before you cast your lot
Could there be something you might have forgot?

There are many diseases that are hard to predict
Some of their symptoms are hard to pick

Study your patient; learn all that you should
You want to be right and not misunderstood

The rule of thumb is the patient knows best
I still think it's wise to double-check your test

So when you decide you have done all you can
You have helped your patient to understand

BEACH

I gaze upon the ocean and hear the wild waves roar
It's such a peaceful feeling to walk along the shore

As I walk about the beach on a clear and sunny day
I sink into another world as my mind is carried away

The seagulls fly so high and soar so gracefully
I feel a thirst for wonder as the magic comes over me

The ocean air is so cool, pure, and clean
It could never be duplicated by any manmade machine

The wind, it blows steady and freely toward the sea
The water goes forever as far as one can see

I want to share this blessing with all whom I love and know
So they can have the feeling and never let it go

Together we will float along the golden sand
Far away from a reckless world that doesn't understand

BELIEVE IN THE MIRACLE

Some things happen we can't control
The harder we try; the worse things go

It seems so impossible to find the right way
We struggle for answers both night and day

We must believe in the miracle with all of our heart
The Lord has been with us from the start

Great things will happen from the faith that we show
The Lord can work wonders far greater than we know

All we can do is hope for the best
For God will be there to handle the rest

The problems we encounter help us to grow
We learn and become wiser than we ever could know

Each night as I pray I hope that I'll be
A much stronger person who lives to be free

Driving with Others

To drive a car equals independence
The choice to go where you can
Along comes responsibility and liability
That can put you on a different plan

What do you do when it's no longer safe
To drive your car anywhere?
How hard it must be to hang up your keys
To show other drivers you care

Some say it's safe to drive just a little
As long as it's a familiar place
How do you decide how little is too far?
Not everyone has the same case

If you are driving because you can't let it go
Think hard before you decide—
Are you doing what's best for others
Or is it just a matter of pride?

Choose wisely, my friend, as you sit in the car
Which side you will sit on today?
Will you be cautious and safe for others
Or let reason be thrown away?

The Burden We Carry

Share the burden we carry
To lift the weight off our souls
Help us find the humble way
To conquer the troubles we know

Worries can be a heavy weight
Loading us down with pain
We must find a way to free ourselves
There is so much we can gain

Don't stand alone in this work
Remember who's by your side
The Lord will always be there for you
With his arms open wide

You can't fail in your mission
To be free from so much strife
The Lord is here to save you
He'll be here throughout your life

You need to hold your ground
Even when you're feeling low
Be there for those who love you
And your faith will make you whole

CARRY YOU SO FAR

Fear is a powerful feeling
We all have to face each day
It takes control of what is real
We run when we should stay

To be afraid means weakness
In so many people's minds
Fear takes ahold and won't let you go
Your courage is so hard to find

You can't go away from your fears
No matter what people say
You must turn around and face it
Instead of just running away

You're haunted by things from your past
That scare you for what you might do
You must avoid that wrong path
And trust you will make it through

So face your fears always
Expose them for what they really are
Then show some heart and courage
It will carry you so far

Change

There's one thing about life that might be strange
Nothing stays the same; it always will change

Whether at work, at home, or out on the street
Something will happen to change the beat

If you count on someone to be there for you
Don't be surprised if they disappear too

We all need a change now and then
But it happens too often again and again

You can't always see it coming your way
But when it happens, it'll change your day

You thought you had it all figured out before
Then the unexpected will come knocking at you door

CHRISTMAS MEMORY

Many years have passed me by
Christmas has shared them all
This joyous season a special time
Of fond memories I still recall

The faces the names the places I have been
all lost in my quick growing past
But a gentle reminder of Christmas before
Renews a great joy that will last

Sparkle, glitter, toys, and treats
come so quickly then are gone
But the true message that Christmas brings
Will eternally live on

Joy, peace, and goodwill to all
A special gift from God above
To help remind us of Christmastime
And fill our hearts with all God's love

CHRISTMAS TO TREASURE

I think of the Christmases I had before
I cherish the memories my heart wants to store

When I was young I was filled with dreams
The magic of Christmas would make my eyes gleam

When Christmas comes I glow with zeal
There is a special joy that we all feel

I treasure the love that this day brings
And look forward to the songs we sing

The deep warm feelings of the pure white snow
Will travel with me whereever I go

Christmastime is a great time of year
The children are happy that Santa is near

Have a great time as you deck the halls
And try to be cheerful and kind to all

Cost of Gas

A trip to the gas pump is a pain in the neck
The price is so high you need a reality check

Gas is so expensive every single day
Especially when you can't afford to pay

Without the gas, you can't run your car
Without a car, you won't get far

You can take the bus or train
And if it's a long trip, you can catch a plane

Whichever you choose, it is going to cost you
So go buy the gas—what else can you do?

DEMENTED

When will it darken?
Either day or night—
My eyes are wide open
Where is my sight?

How can I touch you
If I don't know the way?
Why did you leave me?
You promised to stay

Who do I hear now?
Where do I go?
Was I just there?
Does anyone know?

I have a question—
The answers are not there
Does anyone hear me?
Are there people who care?

The light is still fading
I will lose what is mine
No one to help me
My soul cannot shine

Don't Lose Hope

Down and out is the story of many
To many I must say for today
What can we do to help with this plight?
It will only get worse in every way

Unemployment figures are way too high
Jobs are not easy to find
Finding a good job is like winning the lottery
The world is in need of a sign

How can we turn our economy around
What miracle do we have to do?
People are struggling in so many ways
Bankruptcy can only help a few

Don't lose hope—we're not here to fail
We got ourselves into this mess
If we work hard, we can find a way
It will not be easy I confess

Take a step forward; we can't fall behind
Together we know we can win
We have to acquire the right frame of mind
We must fight for our rights to the end

DREAM TO BE FREE

A dream is something that we think is real
It feels like it's happening to us
A dream can answer all kinds of questions
And put us on the right course, I trust

Sometimes a dream is a goal in our lives
A goal that we must achieve
And if we work hard every day and night
we will accomplish all that we believe

Believe in ourselves and others who can help
We count on them showing the way
when they step forward and do what they can
We should listen to all that they say

Ultimately the work falls on ourselves—
That is how it was meant to be
So we must move onward and do our best
With success we will always be free

EACH STEP WE TAKE

Traveling down a long lonely road
It may seem like no one cares
But when someone helps you carry the load
The trip is light to bear

Each step we take, if on our own
The journey appears undone
There is no need to cry or moan
Together you are more than one

Do not fret if another is near
To lend you a helping hand
Be thankful for the one so dear
Who will truly understand

No matter where you go or where you have been
Our Lord is always there
To help you have the strength within
Your burdens he will share

Early Onset Dementia

Being young is such a treat
I feel strong in body and mind
There is a disease that takes that away
Your memories and thoughts are hard to find

There's not much you can do
I guess there is no cure
You can take the pills and patches
They can help you to endure

When you give it a lot of thought
It really doesn't seem fair
There's not much that you can do
But lean on those who care

Some will ask, what can we do?
This doesn't seem very right
Can't you give it all you can
You have to put up a fight

As for me, what will be will be
I'll live my life the best I can
I needn't fear—what good would it do?
I must do my best to understand

EARLY ONSET

One in a thousand are diagnosed each year
It seems kind of scary; I guess it is rare

Why did this disease come my way?
Was it bad luck or just a bad day?

They say that my family could be on the same course
I must try not to worry—that would just make it worse

I should ponder the path that I am now on
But keep myself going till my options are gone

I will cherish each moment as if it were my last
And look to the future and not dwell on the past

EARTHQUAKES

Earthquakes are a threat to us all
They bring destruction wherever they fall

You can't really stop them when they start
There's nothing you can do unless you act smart

When things start shaking, you're in for a ride
Drop low and cover your head—don't try to go outside

Stay away from the windows; they can explode
Watch for your children and help all of the old

Try not to panic; stay as calm as you can
It's always important to have a family plan

When you go outside, be careful where you walk
You must be prepared for many aftershocks

Make sure you have turned off all of the gas
If a fire starts, be prepared for a huge blast

Be glad you survived for God is not gone
He will be there to help as you start to move on

EASTER

Each year we celebrate in a special way
When the Lord rose from the dead on Easter day

For some it's a fun day filled with cheer
And the money that's spent helps business each year

We must try to remember what happened that day
And worship our Lord in every way

Death is denied its awful sting
For all will rise to shout and sing

Glory to our Lord, our Redeemer and King
For resurrection brings immortality to everything

Life become new; no one's a slave
We will live again as we rise from the grave

The Lord will reign with power and glory
He will show us all mercy as we share our story

Judgment will come as he reigns from above
A kind and dear Savior who knows only love

Eyes of the Lord

It's not the fall that causes the pain
It's being afraid to get up again

Some people feel that to fail is to lose
But giving up is the worst step to choose

No one's a failure in the eyes of the Lord
Keeping the faith brings the greatest reward

Seek out his help for the things that are tough
With the Lord on your side, nothing's too rough

Remember to thank him when the job is done
For he knows your challenge more than anyone

Face All My Fears

I'm not afraid to face all my fears
I must stand up tall and wipe away my tears

Courage is something we all need to know
It helps us get up when we're feeling so low

There's so much to do I can't get behind
The troubles I face weigh heavy on my mind

The pressures we have in everyday life
Just seem to turn into worry or strife

So where am I going and what can I do?
Do all of my options seem about through?

Who do I look for? Can he ever be found?
Or will we be there just wondering around?

The Lord is nearby; he hears all my pleas
He has all the right answers for all that you see

He won't let you go or leave you alone
He'll be by your side both away and at home

Fact or Fiction

Fact or fiction—which do you prefer?
There isn't much difference if you need to be sure

One uses fact so the story will tell
But it's fiction by category and that's how it sells

Nonfiction is similar in so many ways
But without a true story it's rather blasé

So which do you choose—the truth or not?
Both can be moving, deserving more thought

Most fiction becomes fact if you have enough time
You'll see much more clearly as it frees up your mind

Does it make sense, all that you read?
It plants in your mind like a springtime seed

FEEL ALONE

When you're standing by my side
With your arms open wide,
Will you hold me close to you?
Never mind what I might do

I am trying so hard to make it
I'm afraid I might just break it
Will I ever see it clearly?
Can you ever love me dearly?

It's so hard to get by
When you know that you might die
Will I always feel alone?
Can I sing without a moan?

I can't remember who you are
The fear I have is spreading far
Will I ever be the same?
As I feel loaded down with shame

Can you help me find my way
As I stumble through the day?
Do I have to feel the pain?
I fear that I'm going insane

I'm becoming close again
To the lonely painful end
I am thankful God's nearby
As he hears my haunting cry

Please don't ever forget me
When I'm gone, will I be free?
When the pain is truly gone
It's time for me to move on

So walk with me a little ways
Try not to plead for me to stay
I'm in Gods hands; that's where I'll be
The heavy weight is be gone from me

Flag of the U.S.A.

The flag is special symbol
It represents a country when it waves
Most countries are proud of their flags
The flag is an emblem of sacrifice of the brave

There are patriots who gave their lives
So their flag can stand tall and sway free
These are heroes we should never forget
Their courage will live on in our history

Some say a flag is just a piece of cloth
That waves in the wind all day
I disagree with all of my heart
Just try taking my flag away

I'm very proud of the flag of the U.S.A.
I will wave it as much as I can
And to all who disgrace our American flag
There is something you don't understand—

You disgrace an American way of life
I guess I feel real sorry for you
For what you dishonor is a symbol of right
Hooray for the red, white, and blue!

FOLLOW THE PATH

Where am I going; where have I been?
Will I ever get there how will it end?

Life is like traveling for a really long time
You make so many stops just looking for a sign

What will it show you? Will you stray from the path?
Your failure to get there surrounds you with wrath

You must calm down and continue your trek
Things aren't so bad though they seem like a wreck

Take a deep breath and one giant step
Your back on the trail, you must learn to accept

That the journey will take all of your life
You will have your share of worries and strife

But also on that long lonely trail
You'll discover that you are not here to fail

The good times you share will make it worthwhile
You will always move forward as you travel many miles

God has been with you all of the way
He'll be there to lift you and listen when you pray

So open your heart and let it pour out
Give praises to the Lord with a heavenly shout

Freedom

Freedom is a gift from God
Everyone needs to own
If freedom is not in your life
You must really feel alone

Freedom is a privilege in the U.S.A.
Hooray for our American pride
So if you decide to join us all
We will be there with arms open wide

Don't take freedom for granted
There are some who don't do their part
Most Americans will do what they can
We love our country with all of our heart

It doesn't come easy
This freedom we share
Many lives have been lost
As it seems so unfair

Those who were lost
Are the ones who care most
They were loyal to the end
And seldom would boast

We must do our duty
No matter how small
The power of living
Is there for us all

Friendship Is a Partnership

What does it mean to be a friend forever?
How do you find someone like that
Is it a bond that will always last
Or is like pulling a rabbit from a hat?

A friend will be there when you need him
Friends will always show that they care
They're not afraid to speak the truth
Especially when it's what needs to be there

Friendship is a partnership
It has to go both ways
If you're needed, no matter when,
You should be there night or day

Remember a friendship can last for a life
It all depends on you
Just let your friend know you appreciate him
Then he will be there to carry you through

Give Love a Chance

Love is more than a feeling
It's more than a way of life
There's more to it than just being married
To a husband or even a wife

Love has a special message
Sent to us from God above
We really don't understand
Until we feel God's love

God's love is eternal
It will never leave our soul
No matter what we do in life
Or even wherever we go

We may not feel God's love
Especially with a hardened heart
We must open up and let him in
We don't need to be savvy or smart

When true love does become a feeling
It will burn deep down inside
It warms your body and soul
Your feelings have nothing to hide

Always give love a chance
God's love won't let you down
Wherever you are, he'll be close
He can make a smile from a frown

God's love never leaves you
It surrounds your spirit with peace
He will be there to lift you
His love will never cease

GIVE OF OURSELVES

We must be involved with the world we know
And give of ourselves wherever we go

It's true what they say—our world is a mess
We must do all we can to find our success

Be in the world but not of its ways
Take that leap of faith when your mind wants to stay

Give to others all they might need
If you're not involved, you won't succeed

You must believe in what you know to be true
And exercise faith when the Lord calls on you

Be true to the choices that are straight and pure
Accept the great challenge that you're called on to endure

God Loves Us All

God loves us all more than we know
His spirit is with us wherever we go

We can't see God in his perfect form
When he is near we always feel warm

He teaches so gently to love all we can,
To do what is right, and follow his plan

It won't always be easy, the challenges we'll face
He'll be there to help us and fill us with grace

He has given us a tool to help us be free
When we need him we should fall to our knees

The answer will come when it's the right time
He will shower us with blessings we know are sublime

Good Days

Don't count your days; make your days count
If you do this, your troubles won't mount

Each day passes by—some good and some bad
We enjoy being happy and don't want to be sad

Every day is a new day—that's how it should be
If you look for the bright side clearly you'll see

When those bad days come rolling around
Try to be happy; don't let yourself get down

A good day is worth all the effort you do
Remember the Lord will be there for you

He knows how to turn the bad into good
So it's time to cheer up; live life like you should

Good Hard Work

It takes a lot of energy to work every day
Especially for those who only want to play

Strength is needed to work very hard
Like mowing the lawn and weeding the yard

Some people have talents for different kinds of work
When outside of their zone, they feel like jerks

You must put your best foot forward in the labors you do
Keep a good attitude till your chores are all through

Sometimes you must work all alone
To give it your best and stay off the phone

Show up a little early and leave a little late
Most of all don't let the boss have to wait

GRATITUDE

Sometimes it's hard to be grateful each day
What if our life doesn't go the right way?

Showing gratitude is no easy task
But when I need a blessing, the Lord is the first one I ask

Being grateful to the Lord should be easy to do
You can pour out your problems and he'll take care of you

Giving thanks for the good and all you possess
I sometimes forget to do, I must confess

The Lord can read your heart better than anyone can
He knows when you're thankful and he understands

But it's good to give thanks in a short little prayer
That's the least you can do to show that you care

Guilt

Guilt is a burden we all have to bear
It's a trial that with others we often share

How do you feel when you do something wrong,
Especially when it haunts you your whole life long?

Guilt equals pain in many ways—
The guilt may leave you, but the pain usually stays

Can you be free of this awful pain
Or will the curse come back again and again?

Repent of your wrong; you might have some peace
If you don't deal with it now, the pain will increase

I Hate Being Sick

I hate being sick no matter how bad
It gives me low spirits and I feel sad

Sometimes the illness has to run its course
You'll have to endure it till you discover its source

Doctors can give you pills to help ease the pain
But a cold or the flu seems to remain

It weakens your body and takes a lot out of you
It can last for weeks no matter what you do

You cough and you sneeze and pull out your hair
You're convinced for sure that nobody cares

Just when you think you're well again
It starts all over; it seems to never end

Help Is on the Way

Help is on the way to ease you from your pain
Your prayers are being answered; your troubles won't remain

Keeping the faith is the solution that you often seek
Follow the Lord's plan and you'll be strong instead of weak

Treat everyone fairly; be kind to all you meet
You'll never be lonely; your life will be complete

Be a good example and show people that you care
Help and serve your neighbors—if they need you, you'll to be there

Go the extra mile whenever you can
Sometimes things will happen that change the best of plans

Always think of others no matter what you do
Remember the Lord is with you; he'll always see you through

Heroes

Where do heroes come from?
What makes them so unique?
Every hero has a purpose
Bringing courage to the weak

What makes heroes so special?
It's the service that they give
They are there when you need them
They show us the right way to live

They are there to lift us from the shadows
And bring us into the light
They are not afraid to show you
That life is worth the fight

So when you're down and lonely
And you feel like you might fall
A hero comes to the rescue
And is willing to give his all

A hero can be anyone
Who goes the extra mile
Who is brave and kind in all he does
And does it with a smile

Hold to Your Faith

Faith is something we all must have
To make it through our daily life
Without it we would be lost for sure
Surrounded by all our worries and strife

It gives us strength to push along
It helps us find our way
When we're confused and really lost
Faith will always save the day

Faith is a belief in something unseen
It's believing when there's nothing there
You must trust in the Lord in all that you do
And know that he always will care

We are sent to this earth to learn all that we can
It's not easy—it wasn't meant to be
The more you try to understand
The more clearly that you will see

Hold to your faith; trust in its power
The Lord will always be there for you
You are never alone or on your own
When you need him, he will know what to do

HOPE

There is nothing the body can't bear
When hope is there to show you care

Traveling through life can be a slippery slope
Especially when you have lost all of your hope

Giving hope for those in need
Is truly a noble and honorable deed

With hope on your side, you really can't lose—
Things will go right as you learn how to choose

We travel a path that becomes empty and dark
It swallows you up like a man-eating shark

You feel there's no hope; you're lost and confused
This is ever so true when someone has been abused

What can hope do to brighten your day?
When all seems lost, it's time to pray

Hope equals faith and faith makes you whole
It tears down the darkness and brightens your soul

When God intervenes, you surely won't fail
The truth makes it clear and hope will prevail

How Broken Are You

How broken are you? How troubled can you be?
Where is the pain? Will you ever be free?

Where do you go when you need to heal?
Who can teach you to know what is real?

We all want someone to be there who cares
Who listens and stays there and understands our fears

It's hard to forget all the troubles we know
How deep it can go even straight to the soul

We need to believe in someone beyond
Who hears our tired prayers and knows where we've gone

Look deep inside—will you still see yourself,
Or is it another you fear to pursue?

You're not alone no matter where you've been
The Lord will be there for you again and again

I Got Swallowed by a Horny Toad

I got swallowed by a horny toad
When I was just a lad
Now let me tell you fellas
I'm feeling kind of bad

Three long years had passed me by
Before he coughed me up
My girl was wed, my dog was dead,
I lost my coffee cup

Now the moral of this story
Is as plain as you can see:
If you get swallowed by a horny toad
I'll bet you think of me

I KNOW HE IS FREE

It's slow and devastating to all it affects
And takes you in pieces; there is no in check
He wants to fight with all that he commands
But he's losing the battle and doesn't understand

Oh how I wish I could bear his pain,
Shield him from suffering, erase all his shame

Now I am helpless; what can I do?
I will hold him closely until he's through
I know where he is going and soon he'll be there
The Lord will be close to show how he cares

Now I will miss him but I know that he's free
His worries are now over, now what happens to me?

I must go on now that he is gone
Someday it will be my turn to move on

When we unite I will joyfully sing
Surrounded by angels with such beautiful wings

Then we will share a wonderful peace
The joy that follows will never cease

I'll Never Regret

I'll never regret the day we first met
I hope that you feel the same
You're the only one that I truly loved
I'm glad you carry my last name

We were very young and leaned on each other
To get through the troublesome days
Two individuals traveling the same path
We held together in so many ways

We are getting a little bit older now
And wiser in our advancing years
So when things get tougher on us
We are not swallowed up by our fears

Stay by my side as long as you can
How quickly the future passes by
Together there is nothing we can't do
As long as we give it a try

I'm Haunted with Guilt

How can I tell you how bad I feel—
You were so young and so was I
The pain of that day has lasted ~~forty-five~~ *33 years* years
My journey was to go home; yours was to die

Can you forgive me? I've asked many times
How short a lifespan can be
If I could take back what I did to you
I would starve for the chance to be free

What kind of family did you leave behind?
How could I have eased the pain?
Why can't I just go ahead and move on—
Is it your ghost that still remains?

I'm haunted with guilt for what I have done
No matter what anyone could say
I call out to the Lord high above
Forgive me, dear God, I must pray

I long for the chance to see you again
And tell you how wrong I have been
When that times comes I will let out a shout
Now that's when the real healing begins

lon cole

If I could repent and be freed of my sin
What a wonderful day that would be
The Lord could release me of this horrible wrong
I would have joy for all of eternity

In a Hurry

Having patience is easier said than done
We're in a hurry and thinking only of one

Time can be worth more than silver and gold
Especially when you're getting tired and old

I just want it to happen as quick as it can
I've got no time to worry or understand

Too much time is boring for me
The sooner it happens, the happier I'll be

I'm not put on this earth to wait
Nothing I hate more than when someone is late

With all of the time I wish I had
It won't make me happier or never feel sad

I hope to make time for others I see
To learn that everything doesn't rotate around me

Is There More to Thanksgiving

How many times do we say thank you? Not enough I fear
It seems not important though we celebrate it each year

Gratitude is a special way to show others that we care,
To honor our great friendships and learn to always share.

Is there more to Thanksgiving Day than the turkey that we eat?
Can we do something special to make the day complete?

Show the people that we love how thankful we can be
Open our hearts to everyone so all of us could see

Be sure to thank the Lord above for this awesome day
Without his help we would all be lost and never find our way

Thanksgiving has two meanings I hope we understand
We must give and learn to be thankful for the bounties of our land

Each night we should be praying to God who stands above
Then thank him for his kindness and the outpouring of his love

It's a New Year

A new year is finally on its way
What's not here tomorrow is yesterday

Predicting the future is a difficult plan
The world is really hard to understand

What becomes current will fade into the past
The world seems to be moving too fast

We must always keep thinking of how to survive
And learn real quickly how to stay alive

Don't show your fear whatever you do
Remember what will happen is all up to you

Time will move forward—that is a fact
If you want to keep up, you must know how to act

Look where you're going; stay on the course
Don't wander away; you might lose your source

IT'S LONELY OUT THERE

It's hard to feel that you're all alone
When surrounded by so many who care
But sometimes they just don't understand
How really lonely it is out there

I have a family who loves me so
And treats me kind and dear
But they don't know how much I hurt
Or how much I truly fear
Is there hope for someone like me?
Will I ever find my way?
I guess the only thing I can do
Is get on my knees and pray

I will ask the Lord before I sleep
To free me from such emptiness
And fill my heart with no regrets
So I can always do my best

Joy Is Always There

Don't look for what you can't do; look for what you can
Be a positive person and help others to understand

If you look for the bad in all that you do,
Your chances for a happy life might as well be through

Try to smile whenever you can and even when you're sad
Avoid anger always and steer clear of being mad

Look for the joy; it's always there
It follows those who show they care

Be an example of a loving soul
Who radiates gladness wherever she goes

Some will be critical; some just won't care
Don't let that stop you from wanting to share

Love is a powerful path to be on
You will always be needed when others are gone

JUST HOLD YOUR GROUND

What are we doing both day and night
That creates such a hiccup so things don't go right?

How can we correct this terrible flaw?
It rubs on our feelings until they are raw

Can we fight back; will we win?
Or will the troubles hit us all over again?

Don't throw in the towel; you mustn't quit
There are things you can do to deal with it

Tell yourself you're not here to fail
Just hold your ground; there is no need to bail

When you succeed and I know that you will,
Your soul will have joy; your heart will be filled;

Your fear will be gone; the Lord's strength will be near
Others will see you and know that you care

The Lord will be happy as you feel the same
You will shout out hosanna to the Lord's holy name

Keep It Clean and Pure

Nature is a gift from God's great hand
It's the purest form of living that we can understand

He puts it close, within our reach, so we enjoy its awe,
Its grandeur, and its majesty, both large and even small

What a responsibility we have to treat this gift with care
Be thankful for all we see; show respect for all that's there

Don't abuse what God has made; keep it clean and pure
Be aware of all we do or this treasure will disappear

Only man can cause its fall; it's more fragile than you think
A little change can help it rise or quickly start to sink

Gaze in wonder for all you can see
Give God your thanks and be the best you can be

Know What's Real

Memories are forgotten
Too much goes on inside
The mind is always searching
My thoughts could never hide

I want to be alone now
How lonely do I feel?
I long to find my freedom
I need to know what's real

Take my hand and guide me
Help me seek the way
I am not afraid now
As long as you will stay

I have no secrets to share
My life's an open book
The path I travel is so narrow
Come and take another look

Knowledge Is Freedom

Be smart and wise as you live out your days
A quick mind will be helpful in many ways

Learn all you can, don't run away from school
A good education makes you nobody's fool

Read all you can and learn to love books
It's okay to be smart; don't care how it looks

Train yourself in how to become wise
Knowledge is freedom and that is no lie

Share with others all that you've learned
They will help you succeed when it is your turn

Try to remember there are people smarter than you
Not everything you learn will be easy to do

LIFE GOES ON

As the world turns, life goes on
We keep on going till our troubles are gone

What can we do when the future becomes the past?
Where would we go; how long would we last?

Who's there to help us besides our true friends?
They will always be there to the very end

So many things occurring each day
They come and they go in their own special way

Don't be in a hurry; it matters not who you are
Just take it all in and shine like a star

There's nothing to fear; it's all there to see
You should not worry; you were born to be free

Always live life the best that you can
And always be willing to give a helping hand

LIFE IS A GIFT

When you're fighting a fatal disease
Your spirit can become very worn
Nothing seems to lift you out of the dark
You wish you were never born

There is an answer to all you feel
Your soul just needs a lift
So when you pray very hard
The Lord will provide you a gift

What could this be in such a hard time?
How can I ever feel good?
Give me a clue of what I must do
What have I misunderstood?

Life is a gift as long as we live
We all share the beautiful earth
We are never alone; we're so close to home
He's been with us way before birth

When you feel God's love inside,
Your life is complete once again
Be at peace with all that you do
The truth is life never ends

It's just a change of address
There's still much more to see
Your old tired body is taking a rest
So the spirit can soar and be free

Lift Others Up

Be an example to all that you meet
That serving the Lord will make you complete

It's not just going to church every week
You must do what you can to bless the meek

Be there for those who have no one who cares
To comfort their pain and erase all their fears

Lift others up when they're feeling low
Be humble with your gifts; don't do it for show

Be a good listener as they open their hearts
Show that you care from the very start

Do all you can and ask no reward
Give all your praise and thanks to the Lord

LISTEN TO THE LORD

When you listen to the Lord you must try to be still
Have faith is his words and your spirit he'll fill

The quiet peace we all long to know
Will fill our hearts and refresh our souls

The calm you can feel when you worship the Lord
Is a special gift he brings with his words

The message you need is within your reach
The Lord's sacred words are given to teach

So teach with the spirit in all that you do
God's great joy will be there for you

Don't be afraid if you're worthy and bold
To give all you have as we often are told

Listen While You Pray

When I am gone and you're on your own
I hope and pray you know that you're not alone

The Lord will be by your side all of the way
To comfort you and bless you and listen when you pray

Your children and grandchildren will be there also
To help and strengthen you wherever you need to go

Don't worry, dear, I'll be close by
To lift you when you're saddened or need to cry

Before you know it, we'll be together again
It all will become clearer to you then

Don't be afraid; I know you can be brave
God's in control for all of us will be saved.

Live By the Truth

Be true to yourself and let faith be your guide
Honesty is a good trait to have on your side

Telling a lie can bring you so much pain
You must live by the truth; there is so much to gain

Stand for what's right in all that you do
Your life will be more peaceful in all you pursue

God will remember when you make a wise choice
He will be there to help you as you hear his still voice

Give hope to others so they can stand true
If they need help, they can just lean on you

What else can you do to help find your way
Just live life sincere and you'll turn out okay

Live to Be Happy

Happiness is more precious than silver and gold
It helps warm our heart when life gets so cold

It's not always easy to find the way
And try to help others get through the day

Happiness is something that all of us seek
It helps us be strong when were feeling weak

Sharing with others is the best course
For God is the path to the only true source

Live to be happy as long as you can
How do you do it? By giving others a hand

Always be as glad as one can be
Your soul will be lighter and always be free

Looking Out for You

Why don't you listen to what I'm trying to say?
Why is it so hard to learn when all you do is play?

Don't you believe that I'm looking out for you?
Why else would I do the things that I do?

Try to realize that I'm proud of who you are
You always go the distance no matter how far

Trust me when I tell you I'll never let you down
You're always in my prayers and I'll always be around

Whenever you might need me, remember you're in charge
I'll help you with your problems whether small or large

If you get in trouble and you feel all alone
It only takes a minute to call me on the phone

LOST IN DEMENTIA

I am worried, ever so worried, and it's driving me almost mad
No one should feel so discouraged, though all I feel is sad

There is pain in my body; I can feel it everywhere
It lingers on forever; I think it is so unfair

My heart is so bitter that I cry out for relief
A little chance to be normal is way beyond my belief

All that is fair and good appears to be in vain
I can't even start to focus—it's driving me insane

If I have a purpose to live, it's too hard for me to pursue
Where will it lead me? Tell what I can do

Lost in my kingdom where kings never rule
I can't get my sense about me; I must feel and look like a fool

I'm tired and I'm lonely as time passes by
I would like to start laughing; instead I just cry

I have nowhere to go, though I dream to be free
But when I arrive there, there's nothing for me

Maybe there's hope; it's so hard to tell
I must remember we're not here to fail

Dementia may have me but all is not lost
I will do all I can no matter the cost

Magic of Beauty

The magic of beauty is hard to compare
It's more than the eyes or the long flowing hair

Beauty goes deeper than all of us know
It deals with the heart, mind, and soul

When you measure by character, your choice will endure
You'll discover a jewel that's precious and pure

Natural beauty is such a great charm
If you add being pretty, it won't do you any harm

MIRACLES ARE ALWAYS EXTRA

I have never won the lotto
It's probably because I would never play
I never got rich on a gamble
Or had all my money taken away

I consider luck a blessing
And blessing I've had many times
Miracles are always an extra
They help my spirits to climb

I have always learned my lesson
Too many times I must share
When I fall down, I get up again
The Lord has always been there

You can't get something for nothing
That's not the way it should be
But when you receive a blessing
You should thank the Lord on your knees

Some say you can't be too thankful
For blessings that come your way
You can never pay back all that he gives
You owe him for every day

Missionary Work

Missionary work has always been true
There's no greater service another can do

Sharing the truth is charity in so many ways
You teach with the spirit in all that you say

Exercise faith as you speak through your heart
You don't need to be wise or even real smart

You'll learn many things that will set your soul free
This knowledge will be with you for all of eternity

The lives that you touch will bring you much peace
As the blessing you seek will ever increase

Mom

You weren't there when I was born
Or when I was a little boy

When I graduated from high school
You were there to share my joy

You weren't there when I would wet my pants
Or when my throat was sore
You were by my father's side
As I went off to war

You weren't there when I would cry
Or in the earlier part of my life
You were there to witness the eternal bond
Of myself, my son, and my wife

You weren't there to tie my shoes
Or when I broke my new toy
But you were there to share our grief
When we lost our little boy

And when I needed you, you were there
As a mother should always be

That's why you're the mother I chose
To have for all eternity

MORE STUFF THAN YOU

Sometimes people want to possess what you have
And that can cause you grief and pain
You find yourself getting jealous,
Which could almost drive you insane

So they have more stuff than you
It doesn't make them better in the eyes of the Lord
For what you do with the life you got
Will determine your true reward

And if they do something mean to you
Because they are envious of your skill
The burden will be on their shoulders
you'll be judged by how you feel

Just do your best without any guilt
And hope someday they will understand
So when you're about the Lord's work
You are following the Lord's plan

Move to the Now

Sometimes you look at the things that you do
And wonder how you stayed alive
You count your blessings one by one
Then thank the Lord you survived

You want things of the past to move to the now
And remind you of the feelings you had
You try not to remember all of your past
Especially the stuff that was bad

So many memories flood you at once
You're amazed how you take them all in
The special fond memories are saved for the last
In hopes that they'll be there at the end

You made it through life one day at a time
And pray you'll not lose your mind
The people you love and are so close to you
You know they were real hard to find

Discover the future before it's to late
Reflect on the feelings you share
Give others the time that they need
To express to you how much they care

When you say goodbye to all
Leave them with your love in their hearts
God will take care of all the rest
For the time that you will be apart

MUSIC TO MY EARS

They can hear the sounds of music
As it rings throughout their soul
For the tunes that play deep inside
Will follow them wherever they go

Though their memories may be weak
The joy they hear makes them strong
It opens the heart and enlightens the mind
And the spirit reveals their song

No longer the void of emptiness
Controls their feelings or thoughts
But sweet music rings within their ears
New life can now be sought

Sing out loud for all to hear
As it rings of familiar days
And let the sun shine so clear
As it warms them by its rays

My Lucky Day

God opened a window so I can see
The view was amazing; it's all there for me

There was no darkness to dim my sight
It's hard to describe but I felt all was right

The strange thing was my memory was clear
I can retain the details and have nothing to fear

As I wrote down the words, my energy grew
What I was writing made sense and was new

They say I'm a poet but I wonder why
I just write all the words that pass me by

If they make sense, it's my lucky day
I thank the Lord for all I can say

Nine Eleven

Thousands of Americans died that day
It happened so quickly; they were taken away

I was at home watching it all
My body was weak and feeble; my mind hit a wall

So many people martyred and slain
We can't let their memories go down in vain

Something snapped inside of me
I need to go back and serve my country

I know I am too old but what could I have done
I'll pray for our warriors that they'll take out everyone

This dishonoring deed made by men far away
Will be avenged; I hasten the day

Nature Is Beauty

Nature is beauty in its purest form
As winter is cold and summer is warm

Nature is power when it wants to be
It can roar like a lion or buzz like a bee

There is more to nature than all that we know
It can run so strong and fast or glide ever so slow

The truth about nature is it's here for me and you
You'll never know all of its secrets, no matter what you do

Nature is the freedom that passes by us every day
It serves mankind in so many wonderful ways

If you want to know nature as others have before
Immerse yourself in its magic and your heart will ever soar

When you discover nature, then you'll truly understand
That nature is everything that's not made by man

Oso, Nature's Wrath

The boxes scattered around the land
Are no match for nature's wrath
The power of the mountain
Left death and destruction in its path

Nature shows no mercy
When man gets in the way
It's hard to really conquer
No matter what you say

Humanity is the victim
Who pays the awful cost
When nature shows its power
Its victory is our loss

Men, women, and children
Disappear below the mudslide
Their cries cannot be answered
It's Mother Nature who must decide

So sad it really must be
To bury so many souls
So many are still missing
Their fate so hard to know

NIGHTTIME

Every night is different
Though it might seem the same
The difference may be subtle
It's hard to give it a name

Darkness is for nighttime
As light is for day
Night has its own way to be bright
And chase the darkness away

Cold comes along with nighttime
As the heat in the middle of day
But darkness and cold go together
Sometimes in a haunting way

The evening is known to be scary
Where daytime is known for the brave
Which would you prefer—the warm sandy beach
Or the dark cold shadows of a cave?

No Man Is an Island

No man is an island
No one stands alone
We learn to live among each other
Though we want to be on our own

The world is one place
All humans have to share
So many people wasting away
Too many don't even care

We all need to breath air
And need water to survive
Though our foods are different
We must eat to stay alive

We all have to sleep
Without it, we would lose our minds
Some place dark and quiet
We're always trying to find

We talk of peace but thrive on war
Which doesn't make much sense
Intelligence is something we all desire
But many of us are so dense

Most of us believe in some type of God
Or at least say that he is true
When it comes to living all his laws
We find other things to do

We want to be the best we can
And try to enjoy each day
We are the first to complain
When things don't go our way

We want to get the most of life
Even if it takes a lot of work
We're always trying to be the first in line
And having to wait drives us berserk

To be alive and thankful
Is really all we need
To show the Lord we love him
He will care for all our needs

No One Is There

It's not easy to be alone every day
You start thinking nobody cares
We get all wrapped up in our own worldly ways
We seem to have no time to share

Where do we go when no one is there?
Are we lost to everyone we know?
When you give it a thought, it doesn't seem fair
The pain is so hard to let go

I get on the phone and call everyone
But nobody seems to be home
Where have they gone—are they out having fun?
I feel like I'm all on my own

What can I do to stop feeling blue?
I can count my blessings every day
I can trust in the Lord that he knows what to do
And open my heart as I pray

Knowing the Lord is always on my side
And is there to lift me when I'm sad
I guess I can start showing some pride
There's no reason for me to feel bad

No One Lives Forever

Why do we worry so much about our health?
To most of us it has more value than wealth

When we were young, we could never die
As we get older the thought makes us cry

The truth is we want to live as long as we can
Good health is a blessing to both woman and man

We'll do all that's possible to stay alive
And do the craziest things to help us survive

We're all going to meet a similar fate
Some may be in a hurry; as for me, I would rather wait

No one will live forever; this I know
But most of us are in no hurry to go

I know that God has chosen that special day
I hope that I'm ready when I pass away

Ojisan

Being a grandfather is an amazing thing
Kids will wear you out or make your heart sing

Grandchildren are a special gift from the Lord
They can make your life busy and you'll never get bored

Each little soul has its own way to be
Kids laugh when they're happy and they love to be free

They are kids of all sizes from two years to eighteen
Of course they're the best-looking grandkids I've ever seen

Their zest for life is addicting for some
That's why their granddad sometimes acts dumb

Whatever it takes to get them to smile
They're precious and loving without one ounce of guile

I love my own children for all that they do
In sharing their children, their love carries through

OUT OF CONTROL

When you're frustrated and out of control
Calming down is the least thing to know

Just take a deep breath and hope that you'll cool
Before you do something that labels you a fool

Losing your temper can bring you much grief
You may even do something that violates your belief

You have to settle down as quick as you can
Then hope those you offended will understand

Say that you're sorry for all you have done
Then ask for forgiveness from everyone

Don't be afraid of what they might say
Just take it all in and call it a day

OUTSIDE THE BOX

Think outside the box
When living life each day
Nothing has to be normal
Or happen in a certain way

Every day's a new day
There is so much to share
Whatever gives you happiness
Decides for you what's fair

No one needs to control you
Don't let your self feel low
Walk into the sunlight
Watch your spirit grow

When is seems to conquer you
Know you still can win
Stand up when you start to fall
And fight it to the end

PANIC

I know fear; it percolates in my soul
Over and over, it lifts its awful head
As I try to free myself, there's nowhere to go
Now engulfed in fear, I panic instead

I need someone to come to help me be free
Alone I will lose the fight
I need a champion to be here with me
I know what I'm thinking is right

Maybe my cure is a spiritual thing
Maybe my Lord is nearby
When I'm not alone, my heart wants to sing
It becomes easier to laugh than to cry

I'm surrounded with peace; how good it feels
No longer the fear comes near
I've discovered courage I know it is real
Adios to all of my fears

Patches to Wear and Pills to Take

Smoking can become a habit
That will shorten your life for sure
As you're coughing and have shortness of breath
It becomes so hard to endure

The smoke sticks to your clothing
And gives off an unpleasant smell
Whatever you do, it won't go away
You breathe like you're climbing a hill

There are patches to wear and pills to take
That will help you give quitting your best
You must be determined to conquer it all
You must fight with all of your zest

You can win the battle
No matter how hard it seems
You will discover a true freedom
Beyond your wildest of dreams

The best way to stop smoking
Is to never to start at all
And if it becomes a problem
Then it's time to give us a call

We'll be there if you need us
No matter how hard it can be
To rescue you from disaster
And help you to learn and to see

PEACE OF MIND

War is not the worst that we have seen
But it brings out the terror of man
It closes the door on what we call peace
And leads us on a road we don't understand

But yet we fight on
Though it may seem unfair
For those who love war
They really don't care

The Lord is our only hope
Without him we're lost
Still we must stay on course
No matter what the cost

So cling to peace, live for peace
It's the only true path we'll find
And trust in the Lord; he won't let you down
At least you will have peace of mind

PETS

When you get a chance
To give a pet a home
You can always say no
And find yourself alone

A pet becomes a friend
Loyal to all you do
A pet tries to warm your heart
And will always count on you

It takes time and effort
And can be a lot of work
In return pets will love you
And put up with all your quirks

All pets have a purpose
Their master is the one they serve
If you are lucky to have one,
It's probably more than you deserve

Choose your pet wisely
Find your common ground
You will truly miss your pet
When it is not around

Prayer

A prayer in your heart will help you be strong
It frees you from worries or what might go wrong

Each time that you pray silently or on bended knee
The Lord will prepare you to be the best you can be

Prayers are a blessing to show that he cares
The Lord is close beside you; he will always be there

We all want our prayers to be answered right away
Sometimes it takes longer than one night or day

But when you need him, he won't let you down
He hears all our prayers; he's always around

Always be thankful when you offer your prayer
Then listen real closely to what he will share

It isn't important to have your prayer be real long
A short simple prayer will not be wrong

However you pray, it must come from the soul
You must pour out your heart; that's when you will know

Know that he loves you in every way
For prayer is just one way to show you obey

PROUD

Have you ever been proud of something you have done?
No one else can do it; you're the only one

You get a strong sense that you've done something right
It touches your heart the more that you write

Will others like it or think it's okay?
Or will they just read it and throw it away

Writing a poem is not an easy task
You write what's inside of you and take off the mask

Then when you're all done, there's nothing to hide
You've let it all out but can you take pride?

Will they accept the words that you share?
They should start to feel better is all that I care

What else can I do but let it all out?
If I do right, I can let out a shout

REACH OUT TO OTHERS

When you feel your all on your own
Try to remember you are not alone

Though you may be lonely and feeling blue
There's always someone that cares about you

Those little sad feelings you have inside
If your not careful they can grow to be wide

Reach out to others whenever you can
They are there to help you to understand

Don't let the darkness surround you complete
Sadness and depression can always be beat

A smile is the protection you might need
It can be evergrowing like a beautiful seed

Always have a happy thought stored away
So you are prepared for a dark rainy day

REJECTION

Rejection is a painful experience
It leaves you discouraged and hurt
Some say it can pierce your very soul
It makes feel you lower than dirt

What do you do when someone turns you down?
Where do you go to feel good?
Who is there to offer help?
People just don't act like they should

I am sorry I asked for help
I'm more sorry you turned me away
I was hoping you could give me a hand
You could have easily made my day

If you are told "no" too many times
You think you're all on your own
When that happens you're on your way down
You feel horrible and alone

Some people turn out better
They become stronger and learn to be wise
When they overcome the feeling of failure
You can see the glow in their eyes

In each and every rejection
you must always give hope a chance
We are given our trials to be better
It's our right to take a stance

RENEWAL OF SPIRIT

Is our challenge in life hard to share?
Can it be more than our troubles can bear?

How do we find the relief we so need?
The answers aren't easy, I must concede

Where do we turn to find our way?
Is there no end to an awful day?

I seek his soothing and healing embrace
I must find the Lord; there's no time to waste

I drop to my knees and plead with my heart
I open with "My Father" before my prayer starts

I know he will hear me; he always does
I thirst for his wisdom and stand strong for his cause

My burdens are lifted; my joy is so real
The Lord has renewed my spirit and zeal

How free I do feel? My troubles are gone
Erased by his mercy, I now can move on

SAD BUT TRUE

Life is such a puzzle
No matter how hard we try
We forget almost every day
And find ourselves wondering why

How can we get our memories back?
It tries us all so much
We wonder more than we can say
And long for someone's touch

We move about ever so slowly
Our joints are stiff with pain
And when we look, it's hard to see
Confusion is all that remains

Why has this happened to me?
Did I do something bad?
I sit alone and wonder why
My future seems so sad

It's not the trials
That I must bear
It's that lonely feeling
That no one is there

Please don't forget me
I need all of your love
Pray for me my days are short
So soon I will be with God above

Second Son

Several years ago, my second son was born
He left this world in just two days and we were left to mourn

There's no pain that is close to losing someone you love
You cry so hard and then you weep and plead to God above

You ask, why did it happen to me?
You never find the answer that will set you free

I must find the help that only God knows
That healing love that he will always show

I know deep down inside my son isn't gone
He's waiting as a spirit for us to move on

The day will come when we will unite
If I live a good life, everything will turn out all right

How will I feel? What would I say
When I see my son on that special day?

Together again with my second son
One eternal family with everyone

SERVICE

When you do something for someone you know
It opens a door and your spirit starts to glow

Helping a stranger is service at it best
When you're called on to serve, there's no time to rest

The best way to serve is with your heart open wide
You should give all you can without showing pride

You do what you must to help them get by
Easing their pain so there's no need to cry

Call out to the Lord and ask him the way
He will show you the path you must follow each day

Take the great leap where others won't go
Trust in the Lord; he'll reach into your soul

Sharpen Your Skills

I'm looking for the best in you
The harder you work, the better you'll do

Go for the gusto; accept the results
Rise to the challenge, no matter how difficult

Aim for the target that seems far away
Aim a little higher and you'll be okay

Don't be afraid of the trials you endure
They'll make you stronger; your spirits will soar

Take a step forward; be the best that you can
Learn from your mistakes and follow a plan

When you succeed—and I know that you will—
Take it all in, then sharpen your skills

Show No Regrets

To be healthy is a dream come true
Living healthy is not as easy to do

We run, we diet, we get lots of rest
In hopes we can perform to our best

one thing I know that you must never forget
Believe in yourself and show no regrets

It's not how you look or really what you eat
It is going for the win when you face defeat

Becoming fit is good for the soul
Gaining wisdom should be your first goal

Now that I am older the best thing to be
Is a life with balance, for this makes you free

SIMPLE THINGS

As I stroll upon the sand
A peace comes over me
All of nature so pure and grand
As far as eyes can see

The beauty of the rolling sea
As the sunset lights up the sky
The sound of waves so close to me
A joy that makes me cry

The lonely feeling I have inside
Is soothing to my soul
I have no fear I must confide
What more could I want to know?

Is this a dream and not for real?
I dare to say for sure
So perfect is the joy I feel
The memory reigns so pure

God creates such simple things
To touch our humble minds
My thoughts are open; I want to sing
As I leave my troubles behind

So Powerful

It's so powerful how things can be
We search for the answer, but it's so hard to see

We ask for some help to focus our minds
The path moves forward while we are left behind

We were not born as losers, though life may seem small
In each is a champion to show strength and stand tall

Look for courage; find all that you can
Join with the others to make your great stand

Spirit to Sing

A darkness comes and goes in life
Sometimes the darkness stays
The sting of death is hard to take
It comes in different ways

One thing, for sure, death will arrive
What can you do to be prepared?
Just listen to that still small voice
And know there is no reason to be scared

When death comes knocking on your door
It will only take a very short time
Before you know it, your address will change
And everything will fall into line

All of your knowledge you'll take with you
You won't forget a single thing
When you add it to the new things you learn
It will cause your spirit to sing

Stand for Freedom

I stand for freedom and all that is right
I'm a God-fearing man who is willing to fight

Fight for the choice to be all I can be
A life without liberty is no life for me

I wave the flag of the U.S.A.
It must keep waving is all that I pray

What kind of country will we leave to our young?
Will it be weak or will it be strong?

I choose to be strong in all that we do
I will go the distance for myself and for you

I'm willing to die for the right to be free
If you need a patriot, you can count on me

Step Up and Take the Lead

Don't let fear stop you from getting the help that you need
Others will follow you as you step up and take the lead

So many people want to help but they need to follow a plan
This world is filled with a lot of good people who care and understand

Someone to point in the direction and guide them to where they should go
This leader should have the wisdom and be willing to learn and know

The path they take will show courage; they can do it in no other way
To be an example to others, the leader will know what to say

When crucial decisions become hard to make
A leader moves forward, knowing how much is at stake

STEPS

Are you in hurry to go where you have been?
Is your life so frantic that you lose the path within?

As every step is taken, the weight seems hard to bear
If only it were lighter, lifted up by those who care

Some burdens seem eternal—is this really true?
Or does the wait feel shorter when the chore is almost through?

We must pass the final test to get the grade we seek
And rescue all our worries, though they often seem so bleak

STILL SMALL VOICE

You're never alone when God is near
That still small voice is there to hear

The warm feeling that comes over you
It helps you take the steps that are so hard to do

And when you step out and exercise faith
It sends God a message of power and strength

Show also courage and don't be afraid to share
With the Lord at your side there's nothing to fear

Keep moving forward all of your life
No matter the trouble, no matter the strife

Give all you can to your fellow man
Do what is right, and life will be grand

Stop and Think Awhile

I heard the brother say his prayer
I sang the opening song
But I didn't listen to the humble talks
I didn't think that was wrong

I even bowed my head
As they blessed the sacrament
But on my mind was the fun night before
And all the money that I had spent

When the members got up
To give their humble talks
I left to go to the restroom
But I really went for a walk

I was back just in time
For the closing song and prayer
When the congregation began to leave
I was the first one out of there

On my way out the door
I saw a man I hadn't seen before
He looked at me with a loving smile
That made me stop and think awhile

For what if this man was the Lord
And he came to talk to me
How could I face him? What would I say?
How so ashamed I would be

Then I turned and looked again
To see his smiling face
But nowhere could he be seen
He had left without a trace

So now each time I go to church
I worship and I pray
I sing the songs and hear the talks
And thank the Lord each day

STRUGGLES

Breathing air is a simple task
Without air we could not last

Life has its struggles we all must endure
Without the challenge life would be a bore

Where would we go? What would we do?
We seek the trials for us to pursue

Sometimes we stumble and come up short
Alone we are doomed; we must search for support

Look for the light that shines bright and clear
The path becomes steady, absent of fear

Each step we take pushes us close
We conquer the struggles that test us the most

Will we ever reach the end of our trail?
No it's an eternal quest that we must not fail

Rely on the Lord; he will always be near
To show that he loves you and there's nothing to fear.

Success

Some people live for success in their lives
But they are the measure of that success
What's left for them is a partial dose
Because they failed to understand the rest

Looking for success may be a noble cause
But finding success is the final reward
Learning to recognize success takes a special talent
A gift that you must learn to afford

Holding on to success is the greatest challenge
It requires a lot of luck and doing a great deal of chores
And if the cards all play in your way
You've found something special you can't ignore.

Stay focused and true to the course
Don't let anything get in your way
Show gratitude when you succeed
Thank the Lord each and every day

SUNDOWNING

The sun means day, the stars mean night
I do my best when the sun shines bright

When the sun goes down, my feelings change
Some people tell me I act kind of strange

I can't act straight; I seem to be confused
I don't trust people; I feel I'm being used

The darker it gets, the lower I feel
I'll wonder at night if anything is real

When day rolls around, my spirits are high
If you look in my face, there is joy in my eyes

When the sun starts to set, my soul becomes gray
I wish I knew why it happens this way

THE BEST OF FRIENDS

There are friends that walk the extra mile
When they serve you, they do it with a smile

True friends will be there to show how they care
They will treat you wisely and always be fair

They won't ask for a reward; their service is free
When the chips are down, that's where they'll be

Great friends are always loyal and true
The best of friends are usually just a few

Remember, having a friend is only half of the way
Being a friend makes the friendship stay

The Extra Mile

I know a man that goes the extra mile
His heart is filled with charity and shows he has no guile

He gives his job the very best and does all he can
He takes the time to listen and tries to understand

He shows support to his noble team as he works by their side
They do their job so very well I know it brings him pride

He's relentless in his service to show how much he cares
Though time is so precious, he's always willing to share

He understands the power and how precious time can be
And doesn't waste a minute to care for others' needs

Alzheimer's has a champion who is not afraid to fight
He leads his team of warriors who give it all their might

The One That You Love

Sometimes a sickness seems too hard to bear
Just because you need help doesn't mean you don't care

Caregivers do the best that they can
When that's not enough, they need a helping hand

Bring in the help your loved one will need
It may be a health center that takes over the lead

You still need to be there for the one that you love
Hold tight to the answers that come from above

Some decisions may be hard to make
And sometimes the answers are real hard to take

Do what you trust, is the best way to go
The Lord will be with you; he'll help you to know

The Peace Between Minds

How do we claim the peace between minds?
Who don't think or look the same
Is it a war we don't want to fight?
Will the victory fill us with shame?

It's the same old story all over again
When will it ever end?
It always seems to gravitate
Over someone's color of skin

Yes, we are different in many ways
But so many things we share
It should bring us closer together
Equality helps it seem fair

Everyone was created unique
In the image of our God above
He knew what he was doing
That's how he showed his love

Try to reach out to others
Don't hide in your comfort zone
Explore what someone can offer
Our world can't survive on its own

The Plate of Dementia

Why would you order dementia; it always comes with sides
At first it's a small plate that's easy to hide

As time moves along, the plate becomes full
A side dish can be memory loss so you feel like a fool

Another side dish is wandering when there's nowhere to go
It makes you feel hopeless and it burdens your soul

Sundowning is there to add to your plate
It sneaks up so slowly there's no time to wait

As it gets near the end, the plate overflows
Your symptoms takes over; your thinking is slow

Never lose hope or faith; you have to endure
For miracles can happen; they will find a cure

The Power of Love

Without a family where would I be?
My family members are my life; they set me free

I pray for them every day and night
They give me purpose and help me feel right

Where would I go and what would I do?
If I ever lost them, my life would be through

They are a gift from God, this I know
Each one is a treasure that makes my heart glow

To be without family is a sad sight
We need people to love us with all of their might

Love is an action in every single way
It moves through our hearts and brings joy on the way

What can we pray for? What do we need?
The love of the Lord and a family indeed

THE PRESENT IS OUR TIME TO GLOW

The moment is now and not in the past
The future is too far ahead to know
We must live for today; that's the right fit
The present is our time to glow

It's always been known we can't change the past
And our future is too hard to predict
We must make our decisions when we can
Beware of being so strict

Our disease makes our memories fade away
And the future seems so unfair
But every day we learn something new
To give us a reason to care

There is a way to learn from the past
And not make mistakes like before
We must teach ourselves every day
That life is an open door

Which way we pass is all up to us
The door can swing both ways
How it swings for you may be different for me
We learn a great lesson each day

The Stranger

I stood among my fellow saints
Before our service began
And chatted warmly with all my friends
As I extended out a welcome hand

How great I felt to share my faith
With others just like me
To be apart of God's great work
In such noble company

But then a stranger entered our church
And stood as silent as a stone
Not one of us would great him
He seemed to be alone

I wanted to go and shake his hand
And tell him who I was
But someone else would welcome him
Someone always does

I looked again as time passed on
And still alone he stood
When church gets out, I'll find him then

And greet him as I should

When the meeting came to and end
I quickly left my seat
So could find the lonely stranger
That I had failed to meet

But I could not fined the stranger
My heart began to cry
What if this man were the Lord
A great blessing had passed me by

Then God's words rang out strong and clear
As if it was meant for me
For if you have done it unto the least of mine
Then you have done it unto me

The Truth Will Prevail

Waiting for answers; will they ever come?
Sometimes they arrive too late
Your mind will start to move on
It's so impatient it just can't wait

Confused all so often, what else can we say?
How can we survive it all?
Trying to think in a really big way
But our logic ends up so small

Here comes the darkness ever so near
I must avoid it at any cost
What can I do to hide from the fear?
So many questions I feel that I'm lost

Surrounded by worries every which way
Hoping my mind will slow down
Erasing the reason to smile every day
A sadness that just hangs around

I must settle myself and figure it out
Before I forget what I know
I must not be afraid to let out a shout
The truth will prevail from my soul

THE WONDERMENT OF DISCOVERY

Alone with my thoughts
Searching for why
The answers I seek
Seem to pass me by
Where can I go?
What can I do?
Questions go unanswered
I cannot pursue
Searching always searching
The wonderment of discovery
Lay it before my mind
As I seek a precious find
I'm no longer lonely
Freed by the wisdom in me
My thoughts are opened to the world
My mind is for you to see
What I seek is freedom
Like any other soul
Free to express my thinking
Learn what I now know
Make a choice if you can
To try to understand
The purity of the soul

A vision all so grand
No longer lost
My spirit is now free
Together we will be

There Is Always Hope

Alzheimer's is a disease of the brain
It takes you slowly for sure
There is no treatment that you can take
That anyone could call a cure

Those who suffer from this dreadful disease
Are not alone in their plight
They are surrounded by those who love them dear
And will join them as they put up a fight

There are pills to take and patches to wear
That postpone the symptoms for years
But the progression never stops moving on,
Which creates such horrible fears

There's always hope that the day will come
When a cure will finally be found
That day will happen, of this I am sure
I just hope that I'm still around

I will put up a fight to the very end
At least as long as I can
So when it's over, I've done my best
And so others will begin to understand

There's No One on Earth

The Lord is our Savior; he redeemed all mankind
There's no one his equal in spirit or mind

His power is the greatest of anyone on earth
He came to our rescue through such a humble birth

He sacrificed more than man ever knew
We learned from his wisdom all that is true

There's no one on earth who loves us so much
His powers of healing with one single touch

Where would we be without him today?
His message is the purest in every way

I bend on my knees to thank him each night
He banished the darkness and gives us such light

He'll set a great example for us to believe
He brings only peace; there's no reason to grieve

He'll brighten our lives when he comes again
He'll offer joy and forgiveness for all of our sins

THEY DID THEIR DUTY

A man goes to war and is never the same
Too much to deal with the guilt and the shame

What can a vet say to help us comprehend
There will always be wars; they never will end

A Vietnam veteran is history at least
Some called them heroes; others called them beasts

It wasn't a good war that made you feel right
They fought their share of battles, both day and night

They did their duty to country and all
So many were changed; too many had to fall

Now it's a memory so distant and far
They have the nightmares; they have the scars

Warriors are brave in so many ways
How can we honor them each and every day?

They deserve to be proud in all they have done
It's a war that was lost but the battles were won

Never forget those wounded and
    The ones who survived deserve

TIME BECOMES A PRECIOUS THING

Some things weigh heavy on a person's mind
Like being diagnosed with a terminal disease
You go through a grieving process
When it happens it is so hard to believe

You ask so many questions
The answers are so painful to hear
It brings you into a darkness
You're surrounded with worry and fear

How much time do I have left in my life?
Does everyone I love have to know?
Do I have to keep it a secret?
Will it come fast or take me slow?

Can I overcome the constant fear?
Will it be worse in the day or the night?
I must learn to live every day
To avoid darkness and look for the light

Time becomes such a precious thing
The days move by ever so fast
Will I be ready when it is my time?
Can I keep the faith till the last?

I must remain strong and trust in the Lord
He will always be there by my side
When it's my time to go, I'll be looking for him
He will be there with his arms open wide

TO LEARN AND TO LIVE

Doing for others will help you feel good
Be true to yourself just do as you should

Don't blame anyone for what they can't do
Be sure to treat others as you would want them to treat you

Don't create enemies; be honest and fair
When you're dealing with people, show that you care

Take time to listen and don't judge them too fast
Make wise decisions that you know will last

There are all kinds of people you will meet each day
You can learn from their wisdom and what they might say

Every single person has a gift to give
That's why we're here—to learn and to live

TOO YOUNG TO BE OLD

All of my life I have been told
You act too young to ever be old

All through my childhood and earlier years
I faced many demons and chased many fears

I wondered what would become of me
Would my past be my story? Would I ever get free?

Those days and times are almost gone
I learned a great lesson: "it's time to move on"

Now I face a different foe
It seems to follow me wherever I go

To lose your memory is an awful plight
All I can do is put up a great fight

There is no shame even in defeat
It's fighting the battle that makes you complete

So what can you learn from knowing my life
Never give in to your worries or strife

Tomorrow Is Not Always

Tomorrow is not always
It's often too short of a time
And when the day is closing
The time is hard to find

So fast your life is over
This day becomes your last
Each moment hails so precious
So quickly do they pass

And now you're just a memory
It's like you closed a door
But is it closed forever
Or can you still explore?

So treasure every moment
Honor every day and night
Give life all its meaning
Gaze beyond your humble sight

Travel for Free

We travel many ways in life
To get where we have to be
It isn't always an easy trip
And seldom comes to us free

Every trek has a purpose
Though the trail may be shallow and small
Our final destination can often change
It may seem like we're hitting a wall

When we get to where we want,
Our journey is not always done
Why were we going there? Who will we see?
It's almost like we have just begun

Common sense tells us ever so clear
When you start something there's always an end
In the journey of life, that isn't always true
Where one trail ends another begins

Moving on in life is our true goal
And learning as we go by
Life is eternal; there's so much to know
It doesn't stop when we die

Triumphs Are Small

When I was young, I could conquer it all
Now that I'm older, my triumphs are small

I was light on my feet and could move very quick
To get me to move now takes quite a large kick

I was so very strong in my younger years
The lack of strength now is one of many fears

The power of thought was always a surprise
Now all that I think of I hope makes me wise

I had the speed and could run so fast
Now in a race I'm sure to be last

I've longed to be young; there's so much I'd do
Though I am older, my life is not through

I've lived my life and done my very best
To make every goal and complete every quest

Trust Be Your Friend

Let the wind open wide
Though it blows you far away
Don't be filled with empty pride
Be thankful for every day

Let trust be your friend
As you start to hope and see
You're not here to lose at the end
Just be the best that you can be

Keep your eyes open wide
Look everywhere you can
Think hard from your inside
Always follow God's great plan

You're not on this earth to fail
Or to slip when you start to fall
You must try to fly and sail
As you open your wings to all

Turn Out Okay

In defiance, we're usually there to take a stand
In compliance, we try to do the best that we can

Sometimes we're stubborn and too dumb to learn
When we try to help, the credits we'll earn

You can't make me change no matter what you do
There must be a way we can work it out for you

I know much more than you'll ever know
Your wisdom is there to help me to grow

Whatever you do or whatever you say
I know that the journey will turn out okay

I'll be there for you; you'll be there for me
When we're together there's so much to see

Unlock Heaven's Door

There's one way to help you feel young
It's to live as much as you can
Don't be idle and waste all of your time
becoming like a lazy old man

When you are sick and feeling low
You don't think there's much you can do
Many have learned a lesson or two
If you want, they can teach them to you

Lying around and acting tired all day
Is not a good way to go
Giving someone a helping hand
Brings new life back into your soul

Sacrifice often; there's so much to gain
You can be there for others in need
When you help another without a reward,
It will make you feel happy indeed

Each time you serve, the Lord smiles on you
And blessings are always in store
Giving more than you take away
Will unlock heaven's door

WANDERING

One early morning I went for a stroll
The sun was shining and it warmed my soul

As I walked on, everything was so bright
My eyes started hurting; what a difference from night

Things looked so different; where could I have gone?
Don't worry, I thought, just keep moving on

I'll find a familiar road sign or two
This is not the time to panic, but what should I do?

I started to wonder if I'd ever find my way
How could I be lost, it's the middle of day?

Now I was wandering from street to street
All I could do was just move my feet

It was like a big maze as I walked on and on
Will somebody notice how long I've been gone?

Everything was different; so strange it all seemed
Maybe what's happening is it's all a bad dream

lon cole

I kept moving on as I approached the night
It was getting colder; the sun was out of sight

My body was so tired; when will this end?
I must find my way, I think over again

I'm lost and I'm scared where should I go?
Then suddenly I see some people I know

We're so glad to find you, my friends say to me
The nightmare is over; I'm finally free

WHAT IS A PATRIOT?

What is a patriot in these latter days
Is it someone who lives to be free?
Or is freedom a product we don't have to earn
Is it just like taking whatever we see?

I think a patriot is a rare breed
Someone willing to take on the wrong
Someone not afraid to face his foes
to stand tall, wise, and strong

A patriot is someone who does what he can
Because freedom requires hard work
Sacrifice comes as part of the plan
When called on, he will not shirk

Patriots are not the most popular
Or famous that you'll know
But when asked to serve
They're the first ones to go

We need more patriots
That is for sure
Who are willing to give

And not afraid to endure

I call out to all of you
It's time to carry on
If we're not careful
Our freedoms will be gone

What Is That?

Who am I?
Does anyone care to know?
Are you a little curious
About why I act and think so slow?

What is that? I ask
Have I asked you that question before
Can I remember the answer you gave
With me, there's no way to be sure

Why did this have to happen to me?
I tried to live as good as I could
Things are now hard to understand
I get confused and misunderstood

Where are we going? Can you explain?
I get lost each time I go on my own
I wander about until I start to shout
Will somebody please help me go home?

All I do now is stare into space
As if something important was out there
I'm confused by the answers that are given to me
To be honest, I don't seem to care

Don't feel sorry for the way that I am
As you watch me losing my mind
A day will come when I won't know who you are
A new life you must seek out and find

I will be okay, of this I am sure
Someone will take care of me
We are never alone; our Lord is nearby
With the Lord's help I will always be free

When I Will Go

I went to a funeral of an old friend today
It's hard to accept that he really passed away

So many feelings overwhelmed my soul
I thought of mortality and when I will go

I must be ready for my final days
I need more time, is all I can say

I cannot spend what's left of my time
To please myself or ease my mind

Its value is priceless so hard to compare
I must try to live better and be willing to share

So when it's my time, I'll have nothing to fear
For I know that my Lord will always be near

When Sadness Comes

When something sad comes your way
It's hard to express or know what to say

What can you do to make yourself smile?
I think sadness is okay once in a while

It helps you to appreciate the good times of life
So you can erase your worries and strife

There's all kind of sadness for us to compare
From losing a loved one to being treated unfair

So if sadness controls all that you do
There won't be a happy ending for you

You must find all the ways to turn sadness to joy
By looking for things you always enjoy

Who Shows Courage

Courage is a noble trait
We all wish we had
Sometimes, though, we come up short
That makes us feel really sad

The difference between scared and brave
Is not always easy to show
Someone who claims he is not afraid
May be the first one to go

We all want to think
That we won't show fear
But those whom we should count on
Are not always near

The ones who show courage
Don't act like they're proud
They usually keep quiet
So they won't stand out in a crowd

When they are needed
They'll always be there
You know you can trust them
As they carry their share

Why Self-Control?

Where did we learn to have self-control?
Was it from someone we already know

Do we know how to wait when we can
Or are we impatient and don't understand?

We must exercise wisdom in all that we do
So when our time comes, we will know that is true

Can we wait for the answers and not jump the gun
Are we willing to work while others have fun?

Learn as we're doing the things that we should
Then share them with others and you will feel good

All of that waiting and going without
Will help you learn what life's all about

Don't complain if you don't win the prize
All that you learned will make you wise

WIND BE ON YOUR SIDE

Let the wind be on your side
Though it blows you far away
Don't be filled with empty pride
Be thankful for every day

Let trust be your friend
As you start to hope and see
Your not here to lose again
Just be the best that you can be

Keep your eyes open wide
Look every where you can
Think hard from your inside
Always follow Gods great plan

Your not on this earth to fail
Or slip when you start to fall
You must try to fly and sail
As you open your wings to all

WISDOM

I'm surrounded by people stronger than me
Who won't lead me astray but help me live free

They may be my friends, but they're much more than that
I can learn much from them; more than just facts

Wisdom is something we all need to posses
Which I need to learn more of, I must confess

Learn to listen to what wise people say
Then you'll become wiser as you live every day

Open your mind and let it all in
So you will be able to help others again

Seek all the wisdom; learn all you can
Then share it often, as you understand

Words of Glory

There are some words that say a lot, and do much more
They have a power you should not ignore

Gratitude is one word that shows others you care
It recruits loyalty, that you will always be there

Humility is strength that is measured by time
You show it with action; there is no other kind

Honesty is equal to all that is true
Truth brings you freedom in whatever you do

Integrity is the sum of all of the above
Add one more ingredient and that is God's love

Work Is a Value

Work is a timeless value we do
Some people work until they turn blue

Work is essential to make the world go
Some work is fast and sometimes it's slow

Everyone has to work in some way
There's too many people who just want to play

If you discover how to get out of work
Your time has been wasted; you're just a big jerk

Hard work will provide you a sense of pride
Give it your best; you've got nothing to hide

You can work both day and night
Don't be afraid and just do it right

You Rocked My Life

The love I have for you
Is much deeper than snow
It permeates my body
And warms my soul

All of these years
You have stayed close to me
Our marriage is constant
For all of eternity

You are my life
As we share equal space
I see a pureness
As I look in your face

I thank the Lord
Each and every day
I light up inside
As you're coming my way

You have given me children
Who opened my heart
And I have felt pride
From the very start

I knew that I loved you
From the first time we met
You rocked my life
I will never forget

You're Looking at the Best

There are some people who always rise to the top
They have the drive and determination not to stop

They're constantly moving; you won't see them rest
One thing you know: you're looking at the best

These are achievers in the highest degree
They get things done that we can't even see

We need people like them for our world to go
To prove to the rest of us there's so much to know

I'm proud to be counted as one of their friends
I've got their back, and I won't give in

They're usually well-known but not everyone
They're working so hard while others have fun

They're go-getters from the very start
All that they do comes from the heart

I thank them for what they have done for us all
They help us stand tall when we are feeling so small

Your Loyalty Is True

I could really miss you
In a special way
I have come to love you
Every single day

We take our pets for granted
Though they give us so much care
And when they really need us
We're not always there

Can I ever replace you?
It doesn't feel the same
A new pet to care for
Who will want to play new games

If I treat you decent
Your loyalty is true
You will always serve me
No matter what I do

Every pet we live with
Is in some ways unique
We need to treat pets special
For love is all they seek

Alzheimer's and other dementias Resources

Alzheimer's Association
www.alz.org

24/7 Helpline – 800.272.3900
elHelp
You can call us any time of the day or night and get advice and information about the many issues and challenges of caregiving and about Alzheimer's and other dementias.

National Institutes of Health
www.nih.gov/
NIH's mission is to seek fundamental knowledge about the nature and behavior of living systems and the application of that knowledge to enhance health, lengthen life, and reduce illness and disability.

Area Agencies on Aging
www.n4a.org/
202-872-0888
By providing a range of options that allow older adults to choose the home and community-based services and living arrangements that suit them best, AAAs make it possible for older adults to remain in their homes and communities as long as possible.

Veterans Administration
www.va.gov/
800-827-1000
VA administers a variety of benefits and services that provide financial and other forms of assistance to Service members, Veterans, their dependents and survivors.

Alzheimer's Association TrialMatch resources on clinical trials and research

www.alz.org/research/clinical_trials/find_clinical_trials_trialmatch.asp

800-272-3900

Alzheimer's Association TrialMatch® is a free, easy-to-use clinical studies matching service that connects individuals with Alzheimer's, caregivers, healthy volunteers and physicians with current studies.

University of Washington Alzheimer's Disease Research Center

www.uwadrc.org

800-317-5382

Our main priorities are to find the causes of Alzheimer's and to identify effective treatments and prevention strategies for this tragic disorder. The ultimate goal of our basic and clinical studies is to improve patient care and functioning, as well as to improve the quality of life for both patients and caregivers.

Mayo Clinic Alzheimer's Disease Research Center

www.mayo.edu/research/centers-programs/alzheimers-disease-research-center/overview

507-284-1324

At Mayo Clinic, some of the world's leading researchers are looking for ways to predict Alzheimer's Disease, improve diagnostic techniques, identify high-risk individuals, and develop analytical tools to aid in the search for preventative treatments and an eventual cure.

Young-Onset Alzheimer's Resources

Alzheimer's Association – Younger-Onset Alzheimer's Resource Page

www.alz.org/alzheimers_disease_early_onset.asp

Alzheimer's is not just a disease of old age. Younger-onset (also known as early-onset) Alzheimer's affects people younger than age 65. Nearly 4 percent of the more than 5 million Americans with Alzheimer's have younger-onset.

Alzheimer's Association alz.connected.org
Connect with an online community that offers Alzheimer's support.
https://www.alzconnected.org/

Living Your Best With Early-Stage Alzheimer's: An Essential Guide by Lisa Snyder, LCSW
A wonderful, rich, informative & hopeful resource for anyone beginning a journey into Alzheimer's or related dementia. Lisa Snyder strips away fear and negativity to roll out this road map on how to have the best life and make every day count. Highly recommended for persons diagnosed with early dementia and their friends and families. Available on Amazon, Barnes & Noble and other bookstores.

Perspectives, edited by Lisa Snyder, LCSW
http://adrc.ucsd.edu/news.html
Perspectives is a quarterly newsletter written for people with dementia that addresses the concerns, reflections, and coping skills of individuals with Alzheimer's or a related memory disorder. It provides up-to-date research, explores relevant topics, provides a forum for discussion, and builds bridges between people with memory loss around the world. Individuals with Alzheimer's or a related disorder contribute their perspectives to this newsletter in the form of articles, poetry, or letters. Perspectives is written and edited by Lisa Snyder, LCSW and published by the University of California, San Diego, Shiley-Marcos Alzheimer's Disease Research Center. Robyn Yale, LCSW and staff of the Shiley-Marcos ADRC serve as editorial advisors.

Information page on Lon's roles in various groups and his media information

Lon Cole serves as an Alzheimer's Association Volunteer Partner in several capacities: as a member of the Early Stage Advisory Council (ESAC), Lon's role is to direct the focus of programs and services established specific for individuals and families affected by younger-onset Alzheimer's and other dementias. The ESAC is responsible for the programming of the Early Stage Memory Loss Forum, an annual educational conference that addresses topics specific to the needs of those in the early stages of dementia.

Lon is also a member of the Pierce County (WA) Regional Advisory Council, one of nine council across western and central Washington State created to identify and meet the needs of individuals and families affected by dementia in Pierce County. Input from members about what they are seeing and hearing in their communities relative to needs, perceptions, and potential donors and partners is the essence of the councils. They are our eyes and ears to their parts of our region, helping us to reach more people in more places.

Lon is also a trained Peer-to-Peer Outreach Advisor. The Peer-to-Peer program connects newly-diagnosed individuals with trained persons in the early stages of Alzheimer's or a related dementia who provide an empathetic ear as well as a unique perspective based on experience and knowledge of the Alzheimer's or other dementia journey. Participants can speak candidly and confidentially, over the telephone, with a person who understands what you're going through.

Donation page
Donate to the Alzheimer's Association and help fight Alzheimer's disease through vital research and essential support programs and services. Please select the type of donation you wish to make:
Honor a loved one with a tribute or memorial gift.
Recurring gifts ensure stable funding for our vital work.
Your support helps improve lives and fuel research.
Support a Walk to End Alzheimer's™ team or participant.

Donate online:
http://www.alz.org/join_the_cause_donate.asp

Donate by phone: **1.800-272-3900**

Donate by mail:
Send a check to:
Alzheimer's Association
P.O. Box 96011
Washington, DC 20090-6011

About The Author

Lon Cole is a man of many talents and many experiences. He was born as a bona fide baby boomer in the Bay Area of California. His father had the distinction of serving in both World War II and the Korean War. Service to his country was part of his heritage and he followed the call to serve in the US Navy as a combat medic in the Vietnam War, where he was decorated as a war hero for gallantry and distinguished service to his fellow soldiers. This determination to help others is reflected in the diverse and interesting career paths he has experienced, including surgical technician, police officer, private security, and a business owner and entrepreneur.

His friends and colleagues know him to be a man of great wit, with a happy countenance, and absolute integrity. Lon has faced many adversities in life from a dysfunctional childhood, serious wounds from his service in Vietnam, and many other medical difficulties that have challenged him throughout his life. He is supported by his wife of over forty years, his two children and their spouses, and his nine grandchildren, with one on the way. He has also leaned heavily on his unwavering faith in God and his resolve to serve Him by helping lift the burdens of others.

Lon has also found strength in helping others by writing poems. It started after his challenging service in Vietnam and has continued to be a passion of his in an effort to lift up his family, friends, and anyone who needed encouragement through his poetic words. In recent years Lon was diagnosed with early-onset Alzheimer's disease and has found that this challenge in his life has motivated his pen, and the poetry has flowed freely and often, as he puts his feelings and efforts to lift others into his poems.

Even though he has started to forget some things, his efforts to record his inspirations and thoughts have been more productive than ever. He loves to make people laugh, lift their spirits, and make them think about what matters most. Most of all, he wants people to be alive and thankful for the privileges God has given them. He currently resides in Puyallup, Washington, surrounded by his family.
Alzheimer's and other dementias Resources